My Gift To You

My Gift To You

My Gift To You
A Collection of Poetry on Love, Loss and Life

Eugene T. Hewitt, Jr.

iUniverse, Inc.
New York Bloomington Shanghai

My Gift To You
A Collection of Poetry on Love, Loss and Life

Copyright © 2008 by Eugene T. Hewitt, Jr.

All rights reserved. No part of this book may be used or reproduced by any means, graphic, electronic, or mechanical, including photocopying, recording, taping or by any information storage retrieval system without the written permission of the publisher except in the case of brief quotations embodied in critical articles and reviews.

iUniverse books may be ordered through booksellers or by contacting:

iUniverse
1663 Liberty Drive
Bloomington, IN 47403
www.iuniverse.com
1-800-Authors (1-800-288-4677)

Because of the dynamic nature of the Internet, any Web addresses or links contained in this book may have changed since publication and may no longer be valid.

The views expressed in this work are solely those of the author and do not necessarily reflect the views of the publisher, and the publisher hereby disclaims any responsibility for them.

ISBN: 978-0-595-51393-2 (pbk)
ISBN: 978-0-595-61879-8 (ebk)

Printed in the United States of America

*This book is lovingly dedicated to my wife Alicia,
to whom I owe the inspiration for all that I do,
and to whom I devote my love forever;
and to my mother and father,
to whom I owe all that I am and ever will be,
and for my place in this world;
and to my children,
whose collective heartbeats are my reason
for living.*

Contents

Love 1
A Note About Pantheon Of Meaning 2
Pantheon Of Meaning 3
A Note About Endless Love 4
Endless Love 5
A Note About My Sweet Alicia 6
My Sweet Alicia 7
A Note About Princess Alicia Louise 10
Princess Alicia Louise 11
A Note About Say 14
Say 15
A Note About Distant Land (Sarah's Day) 16
Distant Land (Sarah's Day) 17
A Note About I Want To Be (Gene's Dream) 18
I Want To Be (Gene's Dream) 19
A Note About Start Your Engines (Daniel's Theme) 20
Start Your Engines (Daniel's Theme) 21
A Note About Hercules Abounds (Timothy's Story) 22
Hercules Abounds (Timothy's Story) 23
A Note About Oh, Sweet Child of Mine (Elizabeth's Arrival) 24
Oh, Sweet Child Of Mine (Elizabeth's Arrival) 25

Requiem 27
A Note About Balloons 28
Balloons 29
A Note About Seagulls 30
Seagulls 31
A Note About Keep Plugging Along 32
Keep Plugging Along 33
A Note About Waves 34
Waves 35
A Note About You and I Will Ride 38
You and I Will Ride 39
A Note About So Much More To Do 40
So Much More To Do 41
A Note About No Greater Courage 42
No Greater Courage 43
A Note About The Fortunate One 44
The Fortunate One 45

Meaning 47
A Note About My Gift To You 48
My Gift To You 49
A Note About What You Truly Want Out Of Life ... 50
What You Truly Want Out Of Life 51
A Note About Friends 52
Friends 53
A Note About Moments In Time 54
Moments In Time 55
A Note About Take Me To The Park 56
Take Me to the Park 57

A Note About Summer Winds 58
Summer Winds 59
A Note About My Mentor, My Brother 60
My Mentor, My Brother 61
A Note About Giant Among Men 62
Giant Among Men 63

Serendipity 65
A Note About Parallel Lines 66
Parallel Lines 67
A Note About Mournful Melody 68
Mournful Melody 69
A Note About Nomad, Turn the Page. 70
Nomad, Turn the Page 71
A Note About You Blasted Demonstratives 72
You Blasted Demonstratives 73
A Note About Thank You, Mr. Krassner 74
Thank You, Mr. Krassner 75
A Note About Straight 'Round The Bend 76
Straight 'Round the Bend 77
A Note About To Monsignor, With Love 78
To Monsignor, With Love 79
A Note About God Bless America 80
God Bless America 81

Conviction 83
A Note About Summit 84
Summit 85
A Note About Dusk To Dawn 86
Dusk to Dawn 87

A Note About When Married 88
When Married 89
A Note About Unbreakable 90
Unbreakable (Part One) 91
Unbreakable (Part Two) 92
Unbreakable (Part Three) 93
A Note About Fight Fire With Fire 94
Fight Fire With Fire 95
A Note About A Tribute To Mankind 96
A Tribute to Mankind 97
A Note About Definition 98
Definition 99
A Note About Reverse the Trend 100
Reverse the Trend 101

The Lord's Room 103

Acknowledgements 105

About the Author 109

Love
Poems for a Beloved Wife

**The whole meaning of our existence
can be seen and vividly expressed
in the true smile.**

A Note About Pantheon Of Meaning

There are many viable alternatives for the way we choose to live our lives, this is true; however, I have always desired to have a wife and family, and to be close and share as many wonderful experiences as we all grow old together. Now that my dreams have come true, I truly believe that this is the pantheon of meaning for me. This poem is a celebration of my love for my wife and family. Those of you with big families may be able to relate. The rhythm is a simple one and is Poe-inspired.

Pantheon Of Meaning

Love comes calling,
Hearts are falling,
Testament to love's power.
A minstrel's road,
A heavy load,
Defines one's greatest hour.

Husband and wife—
Glorious life—
Clothed in passion and dreaming.
Children abound,
Angels surround,
The pantheon of meaning.

Dreamers endure
Evil's allure,
Seek destiny's endeavor.
Lasting embrace,
Each face to face,
Move onward to forever.

A Note About Endless Love

This was a poem written for my wife, Alicia. I remember writing the first verse on a card for her. I wrote the rest once I returned home. Our first date and movie was *First Knight* with Sean Connery and Richard Gere. We have always loved the Knight-inspired Medieval Times era with heroes and, of course, princesses. This poem is about love that is offered by both knight and princess and devotion that is everlasting. We can all have this type of love if we remember to always lead one another back to him or herself. The rhythm is A,B,C,B with a couplet closing each stanza.

Endless Love

At the close of this evening
Place upon your knight a kiss,
Or sad and forlorn you'll leave him
Without abounding joy and bliss.
Once done, thenceforth ask him for his key,
And observe how his love for you flows endlessly.

In the tender of the night
Bestow a gentle embrace
Or frail and lonely you'll find him
Disillusioned about his time, his place.
Once loved, seek that which his heart will confess,
And he'll gently stroke your heart with an endearing caress.

In the early hours of morn
Speak warmly of your love.
Resurrect the moribundity
Reminiscent of Christ above.
Once shared, shower him with unending praise,
And listen as he devotes his life and love to you, always.

A Note About My Sweet Alicia

In conversation I have always spoken of my wife as a living saint. People understand immediately how much I think of my wife. What they do not fully realize, however, is that I am not simply administering a compliment, although it certainly is one. In truth, I am really making a statement of fact about her. If you knew my wife, you would understand just how special she is, how unique and how divine. I am the lucky one to share her for just a short time here on earth; I am simply pleading that God will also grant us eternity as well. Oh, well ... at least I can hope. This is one of my favorite poems. I always wanted a poem that would be as special as my wife Alicia.

The rhythm of this poem begins AAAB. See how the B is carried throughout the poem. The poem begins and ends with this rhythm.

My Sweet Alicia

I have a wife as wonderful as Saint Theresa.
I might even go as far as to say she is her equal.
She is petite and smells of Gardenia.
You know her, my Lord; in fact, you made her

And introduced her to me as my wife.
Since then dream beget dream in my fantasy life;
A world of wonder and pure delight.
We have five beautiful children later:

Three who wear the color blue
And two more of the pinkish hue.
Rewards for two lovers long overdue.
Soul mates linked together.

I have this sad truth that I must unveil,
As I believe no effort could thwart or derail,
That which threatens my heart to fail:
I cannot hold onto her forever.

My love walks in holiness and grace,
Signs imbued upon her beautiful face
But it is I who know my place:
I am not her first love, her creator.

As she is born from heaven and is truly divine,
I know this living saint is unduly mine.
I should have been last in a long line
Instead of receiving this treasure.

Once we return to paradise this truth I know
That this saint, my beloved, must be let go
And my love for my wife and my Lord will show
Once she is no longer tethered.

It is my only hope that with sweet amnesia
When in the garden I smell that freesia,
That the Lord has returned my sweet Alicia.
And we'll be happy forever after.

A Note About Princess Alicia Louise

This was the first poem I had ever written for my wife. As you can see, the Knight-Princess theme continues. This poem actually chronicles the time when we began dating on through to our marriage. In fact, the poem was written prior to our wedding. The last verse was important for me because it stated and pledged my faithful devotion. I certainly had great role models for a long, successful marriage—my wonderful parents. We had a special place in Nyack, New York where we met and exchanged roses as a sign of commitment. There we would carve our names on rocks while we walked along a river view trail. The style was again Poe-inspired along with a twinge of Sir Walter Scott.

Princess Alicia Louise

Behold! A young gallant knight
Who sings songs to the stars,
While wishing for his princess,
Who now dreams from afar.
Behold! The young gallant knight
Who soars swiftly on the breeze
And conjures up the beauty
Of Princess Alicia Louise.

Behold! A young valiant knight
Who speaks of love for thee,
Whose heart is all a-flutt'r
As waves of a wanton sea.
Behold! A young valiant knight
Trying desp'rately to please,
And to capture the heart
Of Princess Alicia Louise

Behold! The young blessed knight
Trav'ling o'er the miles,
Counts minutes 'til his meeting,
'til her radiant smile.
Behold! This young blessed knight
With but one chance to seize,
Bravely beseeches the hand
Of Princess Alicia Louise.

Behold! This young honorable knight,
Adorned with bridal beauty,
Now calls upon his honor,
With faithfulness his duty.

*Behold! This knight and his princess
Together carve a niche in love's myst'ries,
And their names on rocks and trees—
He and Princess Alicia Louise.*

A Note About Say

This was a poem I had written for my wife on Valentine's Day. It was a simple poem with a simple rhythm. It was meant to express my love for my wife, but it also demonstrates the need for reassurance and affirmation that is important in a relationship. As they say, in order to grow in love together you must grow separately and individually. Throughout the years when times get tough, it is the strength of two separate people who foster the courage that's needed to move forward with resolve and an even stronger commitment. This was one of my mother's favorites.

Say

Say that you'll kiss me
With your sweet and gentle lips;
Say that you'll encourage me
To face life's hardships.

Say that you'll protect me
From all my earthly fears;
Say that you'll embrace me
And wipe away my tears.

Say that you'll warm me
Like the warmth from your throw;
Say that you'll comfort me
As does your pillow.

Say that you'll forgive me
For all my future wrongs;
Say that you'll cherish me,
Just like your favorite song.

Say that you've missed me,
And that you'll always be mine;
Say that you'll love me
Until the end of time.

A Note About Distant Land (Sarah's Day)

This poem was written for my first born child, my beautiful daughter Sarah. As I write this note she is eight years of age. She is the only child who, when born, was handed to her father instead of her mother. It is something special between us. I was so proud to hold my girl in my arms for the first time; I knew instantly that my life had changed forever. She has since become a magical girl, one sweet memory after another. The day she started Kindergarten, a major milestone all parents understand, I cried because I was proud of her. I also cried because I was scared to death of sending my girl to a "Distant Land." I know I am not alone with these thoughts. It was a beautiful morning and one I will never forget. I am proud of this poem; it's one of my favorites. Sarah is also my little poet laureate. I Love You, Sarah!

Distant Land (Sarah's Day)

He was the first to hold you in this world.
You were his precious, beloved little girl.
Your father loved you with a love so grand,
A love immeasurable to the mortal man.

The day of your first Kindergarten class,
Your father walked you down that familiar path;
And with trepidation and tear-filled eyes,
He set you free amidst God's sunrise.

Step by step along that road
He spoke of promises and dreams untold.
And with a tight grasp on your hand,
He directed you to a distant land.

Yellow transport into tomorrow,
He fought back tears, fears and sorrow.
180 days on Kindergarten time,
Where you learned to count and read and rhyme.

Tempus fugit! As evidenced in this tableau
Daughters, as with time, are Dad's to borrow.
Time eventually steals and betrays;
Reminder: daughters are only ours to raise.

A father's love is unbounded and forever;
It is his gift given to treasure,
As are his words to his daughter:
"I love you, Sarah, now and here after."

A Note About
I Want To Be
(Gene's Dream)

When my daughter Sarah was born I was actually relieved because I did not have a son. I wrote a letter to my father explaining that I wanted a girl because I was afraid that I could not do for my son all that my father had done for me. Since that time God has given me three wonderful sons. I guess God had faith in me. My first born son Gene is the spitting image of me when I was a little boy. It makes you proud to look at a mirror image of yourself as a child. Gene has turned out to be everything a father could ask and hope for in a son. All those who meet him know instantly how special and unique he is. He is carrying on the family name and he is doing it in great fashion. What a sense of humor! I Love You, Gene! Keep flying and remember that I am always by your side.

I Want To Be (Gene's Dream)

I want to be a Super Hero!
Play with me, Dad.
Be a dragon, be a villain
Or anything that's bad.

I want to be Superman!
I want wings and a cape to fly.
I want to leap tall buildings
And touch God's blue sky.

I want to be Prince Phillip
And rescue the sweet princess, Aurore.
I will slay the beast and erase the curse
And save my daddy's daughter.

I want to be the Wiggles
And sing songs all day and night.
I can play the guitar with Murray
And smile with pure delight.

Most of all, Daddy, I want to be
The apple of your eye.
'Cause I can accomplish anything
with you by my side.

A Note About Start Your Engines (Daniel's Theme)

My second born son is a beautiful boy named Daniel. He loves to pretend to be a Dad; in fact, he tells me frequently that when he grows up he wants to be a Dad. I felt the same way. Daniel is the spitting image of his Dad also. Daniel loves his mommy, too. He has been attached to her heels ever since he was born. He is our philosopher. Daniel loves little cars. If he had his druthers, he would play with his cars 24 hours a day. Daniel is our middle child, but he manages to find time to love everyone. He takes care of his little brother and baby sister. He and his sidekick Hopson are a father's dream. He is a truly magnificent gift. Drive carefully, my boy! I Love You, Daniel.

Start Your Engines (Daniel's Theme)

Start your engines, Mom!
I am about to drive fast.
I am racing Jeff Gordon with you by my side,
And I hope it forever lasts.

Start your engines, Dad!
We are about to drive far.
We will drive to Splash Down Mountain
In the Booster Gold car.

Start your engines, Timothy!
We are facing strong resistance.
Gene and Sarah and Elizabeth are gaining,
And we are about to go the distance.

Nothing is better than driving my cars
With my brothers and sisters, too.
So, start your engines ... and shall I mention
How much I love all of you?

A Note About Hercules Abounds (Timothy's Story)

My lovely third son is named Timothy. He is a spitfire, a ball of energy. I think that having three older siblings will do that, as they learn from one another. He is simply trying to keep up with the rest of the gang. Timothy is a very compassionate boy, albeit only two years old. He loves all of his brothers and sisters. He especially loves his little sister. Although he can be a whirlwind at this age, I believe he will certainly be something special when he gets older. He has a big heart for a boy his age. When you sneeze, he is the first to say, "Bless you!" When you cough, he has created the "Cough you" phrase. In the middle of the night he places his arms around you, and if you are hurt or upset, he is often there holding you. What empathy for such a young boy! What I love is his amazing grin. It stretches from one side of his face to the other. You cannot help but share in his joy. Keep smiling, my boy! I Love You, Timothy!

Hercules Abounds (Timothy's Story)

He is motion personified,
And as if energy were his twin;
But he is as gentle as a whisper
With his Herculean grin.

He can be a tornado,
Be the eye in the center of the action;
But he is always acutely aware
When you're in need of compassion.

He can be an electric charge
And send your circuitry for a ride;
But he is always conscious of your needs
When you want someone by your side.

He has the heart of a lion,
And though he may throw caution to the wind,
This boy would always protect you from harm—
My loving, handsome son named Tim.

A Note About
Oh, Sweet Child of Mine
(Elizabeth's Arrival)

When our beautiful little treasure named Elizabeth was born we were so surprised and happy to have a second daughter, especially for her sister Sarah. Elizabeth was embraced quickly by her siblings; they absolutely adore her. She is so smart and quick to learn, this little treat. What a wonderful smile. Elizabeth is such a happy girl, she wears this smile twenty-four seven. She is about to celebrate her first birthday, and she is beginning to mirror her older Sis even more and more. She loves everyone and is certainly loved by all. It will be our privilege to watch her grow and develop into a precious princess. Elizabeth was named after my mother. I Love You, Elizabeth.

Oh, Sweet Child Of Mine
(Elizabeth's Arrival)

Oh, my little sweet
baby petite,
you came into the world so discreet;
and we were all there for you to meet.
You were our special treat.

Oh, my blessed girl,
my whole new world,
tiny and precious as an oyster's pearl;
second daughter with hair to curl.
May all your dreams unfurl.

Oh, my little Miss,
my newborn bliss,
upon your cheek I bestow this kiss.
Greet your brothers and your older Sis
as our new princess.

Oh, sweet child of mine,
my daughter fine,
may your yellow brick road fall in line;
may all your stars and wishes align
in God's grand design.

Requiem

Poems for a Beloved Father

*Pain is an essential component
to the human condition.
In truth, it is the only insurance we
have for reminding ourselves that
we do not have to be perfect and
that the world itself is not perfect.*

A Note About Balloons

My father died three days before his 68th birthday. This idea of sending balloons skyward was a wonderful one, a truly heartfelt one. It was the idea of my great Aunt Margaret who also has a heart of gold. This was her way of honoring his day and memory. She thought the idea may have been daft and almost never brought it up; instead, it was the right thing to do. I do not believe I have ever been in a more surreal moment in my life. It was a tough moment for all of us, but I believe our love was truly sent heavenward.

Balloons

On the day
    We celebrated your birthday,

        We gathered out on the lawn ... to

            Sing Happy Birthday, even though

                You were already gone. Three days ago

            You expressed your love for us, before your
                  Safe journey home.

                      And now we return our love

            To you
            In thirty,
            Helium-filled
            Balloons.

A Note About Seagulls

My father loved lighthouses and I can picture him spending time around them in Paradise. At the wake, the priest spoke of heaven as a different shore. I loved the image and I decided to write a poem which included seagulls. Sometimes I believe seagulls can lead the way home for those who are lost. Now I spend my moments day dreaming of the time I will be re-united with my father.

Seagulls

Seagulls flying free over land and sea
Following a light from a different shore.
Lighthouse shining bright into the final night
Guiding you home to rest evermore.

Anchor of faith, my saving grace
You are captured now only in memory;
There to teach and now out of reach
You exist now in my greatest fantasy.

Seagulls carry me during my reveries
And guide me to my beloved father;
Beacon of hope, help me to cope
Until we embrace each other.

A Note About Keep Plugging Along

This poem is dedicated to the memory of my father. I miss and love him so very much. He was and is the greatest influence on my life. He was the epitome of fatherhood. My father whispered these words to me through an oxygen mask as I was leaving the hospital one day. Despite all that he was going through, he was aware that I was going through turbulent times, and still he was there for me. I will do all that I can to be the father to my children as you were to me. Thank you for the example; I was always proud of you, Dad! You are My Father, My Hero.

Keep Plugging Along

I've been burning the candle at both ends,
Trying desperately to make my amends with you.
I've kept my nose to the grindstone,
And with your guidance I will find home and you.

When the pressure begins to strengthen,
And my fears are too great to mention,
I will close my eyes and think of you
And remember the words you said to do:

Keep Plugging Along, Keep steadfast and strong
Don't let anything get in your way;
Keep Plugging Along, Forgive all your wrongs
Give all that you've got each day.

I will work 'til I drop
And bleed 'til it stops for you.
I will crash and burn
And live and learn without you.

And when the stress begins to worsen,
And I'm not the same old person,
I will remember the day I spent with you
When you whispered the words you said to do:

Keep Plugging Along, rise above each storm
And let your own heart lead the way;
Keep Plugging Along, keep safe from harm
And in your heart I'll always stay.

A Note About Waves

Anyone who has ever lost someone dear can relate to this poem. When it occurs to you that the unthinkable has actually happened, it crushes you. What's worse is that the thought of what has occurred comes and goes in waves, but they never stop. You cannot turn them off. Even when you think you are prepared for the inevitable, you soon learn you are not. And then the waves continually torment you and remind you of what you have lost. We only hope at some point to ride these waves in a different, more forgiving and hopeful way.

Waves

The moment I learned I lost my father,
was like no other.
It was a suffering matched by no other grief.
It shook my faith and all my beliefs;
Grim Reaper is the ultimate thief!
Don't fear the reaper; fear instead the waves!
Every other moment you're reminded of the grave.
No sense in being brave—with waves, you're going to cave.

I am lost at sea, thinking of you and me,
Wishing we had more time together.
I am lost on the ocean, riding waves of emotion,
Holding onto memories of you forever.

These waves of a wanton sea
have no compassion for you and me.
They are cruel tides that ride on high
and crush your serenity.
You will see what will be your destiny:
Moment upon moment of misery.
Left alone with your tragedy.
No remorse, No sympathy!

I am lost at sea, dreaming of you and me,
Re-living every cherished memory.
I am lost on the ocean, drowning in waves of emotion,
Missing you for eternity.

In this year of two thousand and seven
my father has been called and invited to heaven.
It is the Century of twenty and one,
and though the waves have had their fun,

one thing can never be undone:
The simple truth
that we were Father and Son.
To that end, we have triumphantly won!

A Note About You and I Will Ride

When I wrote this poem the death of my father was fresh in my mind; in fact, it was the only thing on my mind. The feelings and emotions were raw, as you can see. When it truly hits home that you will never see nor hear from your father again, the pain is excruciating—it's on a completely different level. Life, as you have known it, has changed forever! Your childhood seems misplaced; you are forever on your own now, and it's up to you. This is a frightening reality. Though my father's voice cries silently now, my dream and hope is to ride through the Lord's majestic fields of gold on stallions together with my Dad. God, I miss him!

You and I Will Ride

I have realized with death there is no choice,
For I will never again see your face,
Nor will I ever again hear your voice.

All alone in the reaper's hearse
I must come to grips with this curse,
This mantra, the devil's verse.

Just as the fountain of youth eludes us all,
There is no promise of winter, summer or fall;
Only times we shared together when we stood tall.

With but fleeting memories to enthrall
We are forever left empty, crestfallen and small,
Where silence is your call.

Deflated hope resembling bread unleavened,
We have only the promise of time spent with our brethren
Together for eternity in God's glorious heaven.

Where you and I will ride unbounded and unbidden
Among majestic fields of gold unfettered and unridden,
With treasures exposed and unhidden.

A Note About So Much More To Do

Tears fell as I wrote this poem. I think I wrote this because the tears were falling. These were raw emotions being translated to words in real time. I was angry, afraid and alone, as you can see. My father was too young to die; many of you can relate, I'm sure. He always wanted to visit Disney with my children, but he never got the opportunity. We talked always about different plans and ideas, whether it be about family, the house or whatever. The fact was, we had so much more to do ... together, both as father and son, and as grandfather and nieces and nephews. Wherever we go and whatever we do, Dad, we know you're with us.

So Much More To Do

C'mon, Dad ... are you there?
You can't be anywhere, but here!
It isn't fair.
I am in despair.
I know you care.

C'mon, Dad ... can the game be done?
The game is over, you've won!
This isn't fun.
Now, it is I you shun,
Your only son.

C'mon, Dad ... what is there to gain?
Where is the pleasure in this pain?
This is the devil's end game.
This torment is insane.
Let's start all over again.

C'mon, Dad ... tell me it's not true!
After all, each day begins anew,
The sky remains blue,
And we have so much more to do.
We have so much more to do.

A Note About No Greater Courage

My father worried more about my mother's health for the better part of two decades. Many nights we worried and cried about her health. So many nights spent in hospitals where my father would cry to me and tell me that he did not know what he would do if anything ever happened to her. No one ever suspected that he would suddenly succumb to such a devastating disease. No one, however, was surprised to see our mother rise to the occasion with greater courage and resolve. There was never a greater sign of such love and devotion. I was a witness to this, but I am also a proud product of this, as well. My mother is one in a million—they truly deserved one another!

No Greater Courage

When a wife and a husband pledge a life together,
The heartfelt promise no doubt comes from the heart.
But there is no line in the pledge taken for granted lesser
Than the ominous, "'til death do us part."

When my father was diagnosed with terminal cancer
We had no choice but to encourage
My mother who was left alone with no answer
To summon a life's worth of courage.

I have never been more proud of my mother
I have never witnessed more courageous behavior;
And I am sure her husband, my father
Was grateful for his wife, his savior.

In the end my father reached only for my mother's hand,
During these seconds of such strong emotion;
The rest of us observed to understand
This sign of the greatest devotion.

Mom, you were a heroic example for your son and daughters;
Though you certainly had nothing to prove to me.
My image of you is even brighter and broader,
For I have loved you forever and will throughout eternity.

A Note About The Fortunate One

I have so many wonderful memories of my mother. She is living and has always lived a very quiet, unassuming life. She loves the small things in life: spending time with her family, taking vacations and, of course, shopping. She spent 49 years married to my father before he passed away suddenly. Now we watch her endure alone but with the same unassuming determination she always had. I am so proud of her. She always spent quality time with me growing up. I will always remember how she shared my love of sports with my father and me. She would watch the New York Knicks and actually keep score with me. Anything I ever wanted or desired she gave me. All she cared about was giving and making her children happy. I know my sisters and I are forever grateful. Now we do what we can for our children as she did for us. She loves her grandchildren, and they love her. She is without question the perfect mother, and I love her with every beat of my heart. I am so proud and fortunate to be her son.

The Fortunate One

To use a metaphor: a father is a library;
A mother is a store.
To these notions I will assuredly admit
That they are accurate, I'm sure.

Whenever information was sought and needed,
My father's voice I heeded;
Whenever anything my pleasure did adore
I turned to my mother's unfathomable store.

My mother's love was freely employed;
In fact, it was by no means inhibited.
And no greater joy she ever enjoyed
Than to see the happiness her son exhibited.

What she gave her son was nothing but the ultimate
And neither size nor substance would deter;
For as a mother she was nothing short of the consummate
For giving quality time, words and more.

I have been told by a wise man
That there is no greater love than between a mother and a son.
If this be true, be certain to understand
That I am the fortunate one.

Meaning
Poems for a Minstrel's Road

The purpose of life is to grow:
divinely, humanely, intellectually,
exponentially, gracefully,
and lovingly.
Simply this, and no more.

A Note About My Gift To You

This poem was written many years ago as a message to my students. I tried to instill a love of poetry in my students for more than a decade. Many of them truly appreciated the art, and I hope they were inspired to continue writing. I know their poetry touched me many years ago. It is amazing how true this message is, though. I truly believe we become someone new every time we learn something we didn't know before. Sometimes we even act differently, think differently, and believe differently. Knowledge and wisdom tend to do that, don't they? Can you relate?

My Gift To You

Every time I learn something,
I become someone new.
I'm not the same as I was before,
And neither are you.

Every time I learn something,
I change that very minute.
And I'm amazed to see the world goes on
And that I'm still in it.

Every time I learn something,
I develop more love for me.
I am introduced to a person
Who, before, I didn't see.

Every time I learn something,
I tell a friend or two,
Because all that I've now become
Is my gift to you.

A Note About What You Truly Want Out Of Life

This was the first poem I ever had published back in 1987. The amazing thing about it was that it came to me when I was asleep. Anyone who writes poetry may understand, but thoughts, phrases and images come to you when you least expect them. I remember sitting up quickly and writing these words down. I polished it and it was done. Years later a student somewhere in the country enjoyed my poem and wanted to use it in her high school yearbook. Her mother called and asked for permission, and I was honored and privileged. I was so stunned by the phone call, I couldn't even remember who called or the name of the high school. Well, anyway ... I am still grateful. I am a proud disciple of Leo Buscaglia, a person who had a tremendous influence on my life. I have always believed that love was the means of life.

What You Truly Want Out Of Life

What you truly want out of life
cannot be found in the world,
because what you truly desire,
what you truly long for,
can only be found within yourself.
It does not exist and cannot be found outside of you.
You must search within your heart,
and not take for granted what your heart offers,
for it is the only true messenger that you have.
The heart is the only road paved to
fulfillment, happiness, and love.
For those things that we hold in the
palms of our hands are only as large
as that which we can grasp,
but that which we hold in our hearts
is ever increasing,
   ever expanding,
      forever developing.
It is as large as the world itself.
That which we hold in our hearts
is love ...
the only means of life.

A Note About Friends

My first love in poetry was Poe's "Annabel Lee." It had everything for me: imagery, alliteration, surrealism, passion and pain. With "Friends," I wanted to capture the essence of friendship. We are a composite of life experiences that have been immeasurably influenced by friends and family. My hope is that all who read this poem will relate to the special qualities that make friendship so endearing. This may be one of my more recognized poems, and it is certainly one of my favorites.

Friends

Days sped by, as did blue skies
Beyond the yonder winds.
My friends and I sailed the tides
And survived each day's grin.

We reveled in the joys and laughter,
During those days when our spirits were free.
We spontaneously dictated our pleasures
When we refused to resign to ennui.

Yet there were days when we'd surrender.
Yes, there were days when we'd succumb
To the heat of the fire's blue embers,
Which left our passions numb.

Though, through it all we remained enchanted,
Held aloft by our capricious dreams.
And years from now we'll remain united
By those memories held in high esteem.

A Note About Moments In Time

I wanted a simple poem with a simple rhyme and simple message—follow your dreams. My inspiration for "Moments In Time" came from the poetry of Albert Krassner. I believe regret is a fundamental part of the human condition. Embracing risks and seizing opportunities allow us to have fewer regrets; furthermore, taking such positive actions will transform and redefine who we are as individuals. I hope the simplicity will provide the inspiration for all.

Moments In Time

Moments are essentially periods in time
When opportunities are seized or left behind.
We have only flashes to take advantage of these
Or view the ripples of regret on drifting seas.
Time may be an insensitive master of chance,
A simple provider of daily happenstance,
That offers such freedoms as those of choice
That gives meaning to purpose and sound to voice.
Regret is a reminder of times we surrendered
When moments were lost and later remembered.
In moments of decision we turn to the heart
And listen for the beats of wisdom it imparts.
Uncertainty is the gift that leads us to be
In control of our own hand-written destinies.
In the final analysis, fear is our paralysis.
The answer to time lies within this rhyme:
    Opportunities are to be achieved,
      As is the fulfillment of all dreams believed.

A Note About Take Me To The Park

I remember playing outside when I was young. We would play until it was dark. We played in the neighborhood and we played every game imaginable. Friends were something special when you were young, weren't they? Now my daughter frequently asks me to go to the park, and I understand the need and desire to play. Neighborhoods have changed, and now she plays with her brothers and sister. In our hearts the memories of those times stay with us forever, as do those friends who shared them with us. I still cherish my childhood friends: Jose, Mark, Johnny, Cliff, Michael, Dante and Hyuncher.

Take Me to the Park

Take me to the park
where the winds chime
as echoes of forgotten play;
where dusk marks the time
when children's follies cease.
They make their pleas
to delay nature's shade—
the imminent arrival of a dark descent—
that shadows secrets
and threatens never to reveal
reveries of the young poets and dreamers.
Take me to the playground of the heart
where everyone resides,
sorrows subside,
and the restless find solace
in slumbering minds.
Winds stir
and echoes resound,
and everything is as it ought to be,
at the park.

A Note About Summer Winds

We all have memories of summer and its wonderful experiences. Many of my memories are from childhood and with my family. This poem is simply an ode to summer and to the times when we all yearned to find something to hold onto whenever summer came around, whether it was summer love or a vacation with the family. Thanks to my parents I always had wonderful summers. Now I hope to do the same for my children.

Summer Winds

Summer winds
play their games:
Capricious changes
cover vast terrains;
Welcomed breezes
and soothing drafts
join cooling spirits
and night-filled laughs;
Gentle whispers
above calming silence
blend romantic interludes
with hidden blindness.
Songs of summer,
riding waves of air,
seeking pleasure purpose
and a long, drawn stare.
Summer winds
forever come and go,
as do many fancies
and memories of long ago.

A Note About My Mentor, My Brother

I have had three great men in my life: my father, my father-in-law and my friend, Robert Chomiak. In reference to the latter, my life would not have been as enriched and complete if it were not for this individual. Anyone who knows Bob can speak volumes about his incomparable personality, sense of humor and unconditional Christian love and generosity. He is the brother I never had, and I love him dearly for being an important part of my life. I dedicate this poem to him. Oh, and the stories I can tell....

My Mentor, My Brother

We are selective and guarded when choosing friends;
We look left, right, front and center,
And we are better off in the end
When we find gold and not glitter.
Every person is a history;
Every person is a book.
And while some may be plain and not claim such glory
Others are quite special and require a second look.

The special ones are they
Who are the ultimate plus,
Because instead of we choosing them,
They have chosen us.
And it was even fortuitous
When the one who was to enter,
By divine means circuitous,
Was the presence of a trusted mentor.

In the end, when we reflect on our lives together
And look to the friends we have chosen,
We see that they were covered with neither gold nor silver;
But, rather, gifts packaged from heaven.
I will forever be grateful for all of my friends
Be they gold, bronze or silver;
But I am indebted forever for the one in the end
Who treated me always as his brother.

A Note About Giant Among Men

This poem is dedicated to my father-in-law, Richard Anastasio. He is more than just a wonderful father-in-law, he is a very special and unique person. What I admire about him is his incredible wisdom and understanding of family. He truly understands how fragile life can be, and he wants everyone to appreciate the moment. He wants the very best for his children. He is very sensitive and sentimental when it comes to his five daughters. What is amazing is this great person lives without any extended family—no brothers, sisters, uncles or aunts. Yet, his love for his family and his unconditional love for people is astounding. When my father was on his death bed he promised my father that he would take care of me and he reassured my father that we would be fine. That alone is a gift that I will treasure for the rest of my life, and I know that he was more than sincere, he was and is truly genuine. He is a Giant Among Men.

Giant Among Men

He is a man of small stature
Living without family or lineage.
And he was raised by his mother on the east side of New York,
Far from his Mediterranean heritage.

Born from parents who were themselves orphans
This great man knows what it means to be alone;
And when he was rewarded with five beautiful daughters
He gave more than five fathers and left no unturned stone.

He is no longer a man against the world
As he is blessed with one great quality:
As his heart is as large as the Rock of Gibraltar,
So is his unconditional love and understanding of family.

This man believes the sky is the limit
When it comes to family and his five girls.
And he works as hard as a Chinese Laundromat
To give these five girls the world.

He is a man indicative and worthy of nobility,
And he is a wonderful example of intelligence and acumen;
And this small man who gives so much of himself
Is truly a Giant Among Men.

Serendipity

Poems for a Peaceful Soul

*Joy, laughter, and happiness are
wonderful things to experience;
however, without pain, sadness
and tears, we wouldn't truly know
all that we have.*

A Note About Parallel Lines

We have all had relationships in the past that, for one reason or another, simply did not pan out as we had hoped or imagined. Perhaps it was divine intervention or simply human incompatibility. Sometimes we get in our own way and follow our minds instead of our hearts. When this happens we end up living lives down different roads. It's amazing how we create parallel lines with people who, at one time in our lives, meant something special. Paths that are never meant to cross again. Sometimes it's for the better; other times it's about regret. In the end we all survive and make the most out of life.

Parallel Lines

Once upon a different scene,
We lived as lovers and shared a dream.
Though our hearts beat as one,
Our love fell victim for youth's wisdom.

The same paths that we both once tread
Began a fatal divergence instead.
Young lovers who were each other's first
Embraced separate paths and eternity's curse.

For the union that once bound us together
Is lost in the past and drifting forever.
Two dreamers facing the signs of the times:
Living in the past and riding parallel lines

That will never cross familiar paths again,
As fate—so stubborn—delivers destiny's end.
Oh, but the memories—so cherished, so cheap
Last but only briefly in dreams so deep.

But there is meaning even in love lost,
As it is precious, enduring and priceless at any cost.
What we once had is now but a glimpse in time,
Forever a song with our own private rhyme.

A Note About Mournful Melody

This poem was inspired by a newspaper article. It is amazing how often our stories become inspiration for articles, songs, books, movies, poetry and such. Sadly, we know too many couples whose lives fit this description. We have such high hopes for our relationships and marriages; we are devastated when we find that our bonds that united us in the first place were too fragile. Only the people who go through such a tragedy know what it feels like in the end. The only role we can play is one of support and encouragement. For those of you who have been hurt in this fashion, turn the page in your lives and move on with confidence and conviction.

Mournful Melody

Sit down my friend
and listen to my song.
It's about broken promises
and a love gone wrong.
It tells of cherished memories
and unfulfilled dreams,
unwarranted discontentment
and calculated schemes.
It's a story of disillusionment
that often doesn't describe
the hidden love and passion
that two secretly imbibe.
It's a mournful melody for lovers
whose hearts feel all alone
by abandoned bonds of matrimony
that have never fully grown.
When it's time for curtains to close
and devotions to be swept away,
only the lonely can measure the heart
and the pain at the end of the day.

A Note About Nomad, Turn the Page.

I believe we all feel like this at some point in our lives. You are very fortunate if you have not. It is part of the human condition to feel despair and isolation. The decisions we make when we feel this way are crucial, as they lead to new opportunities and experiences. These new experiences provide moments for us to say "Yes" and to risk new challenges and traverse new frontiers. Remember, everyone is a book with more pages to turn! If you're still alive, if your heart still beats, then you still have more pages to turn. Only the last page reads, "The End."

Nomad, Turn the Page

I'm tired,
I'm alone;
I'm a soul without fortune or home.
I'm lost
In place;
I'm a fragment without substance or space.
I yearn,
I feel;
I'm a nomad who's unequivocally real.

When life turns a corner and offers new hope,
It provides strategies to defend and to cope.

I'll live,
I'll learn;
I'm a book with more pages to turn.
I'll search,
I'll find
That person who is decidedly mine.
I'll smile
And be
Unconditionally content and carefree.

A Note About You Blasted Demonstratives

We all struggle for purpose and direction in life. This came at a difficult time when I began questioning my direction and desires. I had fun with this poem. It is I having a dialogue with myself. Sometimes, like Ogden Nash, it is enjoyable and the poet's right to take liberties with the language. This is what I did here. It remains one of my favorite poems. We cannot beat ourselves up when we find ourselves in need of guidance. I believe fortitude comes when we push ourselves to the limit and the human spirit takes over.

You Blasted Demonstratives

Shall I do this? Shall I do that?
It seems I am against myself in combat.
How do I choose amongst endless choices?
How can I focus amidst perturbing voices?
Oh, you blasted demonstratives!
You confuse me with more unanswered questions;
You maim me with more disturbing doubts.
I sit here aimlessly wondering what on earth you're talking about.
Am I that? Am I this?
Am I capable of enjoying bliss?
How do I the right choice determine
And end the self-inflicted sermon?
At least I won't have to deal with these and those,
As that would only add to my increasing woes.
I'll be satisfied with the simple singular.
Although, what's escaping me is the one particular.
So, this or that?
This is your last chance.
Portrait for me my circumstance.

A Note About Thank You, Mr. Krassner

Many years ago one of my students gave me a wonderful gift. It was a small book of poetry written by Albert Krassner called Soaring. I do not know how many people know of this terrific poet, but he was a great inspiration for my writing ever since I received this gift. His poetry was simple, contemplative and rhythmical. I made the decision that my poetry would have a similar style. He gave me a style that allowed me to feel free in my expression without concern for overwhelming substance. The true gift, however, came from the messages he gave me in his work. I am proud to say that I am a disciple of Mr. Krassner, although I have never met him, nor do I know much about him. Thank you, again, Mr. Krassner. I will carry on your traditions of Soaring in my poetry and my life.

Thank You, Mr. Krassner

Thank you, Mr. Krassner
For giving me the key to life,
And sharing with me your wisdom
For avoiding life's misery and strife.

Life isn't about pleasing others.
It's not about the need to appease.
It's more about keeping my ego in check and
"Soaring on my own inner breeze."

When my thoughts, feelings and anger arise
And feel the need to want out,
I check the need for others to please
And remind myself what I'm about.

I will live my life as free as a bird
And vow to give my best shot;
And when others behoove and disapprove,
I will respond with a healthy "Shut Up!"

Saying YES when I want to and NO when I choose
Will lead to a favorable position;
And choosing my own paths on the road of life
Will make pleasant my disposition.

A Note About Straight 'Round The Bend

Straight 'Round the Bend was inspired by a song by The Fixx, although one had nothing to do with the other. I used the title as a metaphor for our destination after death. The majestic corner sublime represents our death, and some of us may turn left at the corner and some may turn right. I wrote this many years ago, obviously prior to the death of my father. It's ironic that I now read the line, "We have family who walk before us ..." It is important that we recognize that the race has begun; we need to make the most of our efforts while we can. So if you have not already done so, think of at least one fantastic thing you are going to do and contribute to this life. And then do it! That majestic corner sublime can wait ... in due time.

Straight 'Round the Bend

In a single file we walk
Straight 'round the bend.
Whether we turn left or right
Doesn't matter in the end.
We have family who walk before us,
And friends who walk behind;
And with these soul mates we tread on tread
Unto the majestic corner sublime.
There are days we play the follower,
And there are days we're the guiding light.
All in all, we march on and on
'round the bend with the end in sight.
Some may join us along the way;
Others may later enter the race.
We'll remember it was never their choice,
So we'll pardon them with our embrace.
In the end, it doesn't matter how we arrive.
Some may soar, some may walk, some may run.
And it's irrelevant knowing when we'll answer the call,
But it's relevant knowing the race has begun.

A Note About
To Monsignor, With Love

Monsignor Edmund Netter was a very special priest. Those who came into contact with him can testify to his greatness as a person, his devotion to his calling, and his compassion for those he served and befriended. I was simply fortunate to have had a small time to enjoy his company and, more important, his respect. I was too young to appreciate his confidence in me; if we met today, I am certain we could move mountains together, while still enjoying a good dinner, a good film and, of course, sports and Notre Dame. Father Netter, I will never forget our times together; I look forward to our next dinner together at God's great table. Thank you for believing in me!

To Monsignor, With Love

You had a special confidence in me that took years to realize.
Yet, I always knew you were the special one:
The one who devoted his life to the cross to specialize
In bringing others to the Lord, God's own Son.

We developed a beautiful relationship, you and I
We spent every weekend enjoying film and Notre Dame;
However, the years you gave the Lord could only justify
Why you were called to bear witness to His name.

I wonder how many remember your name these days
Or your endless activities with children and those you served.
You need to know that I think of you often and pray
That your rewards in heaven are as plentiful as deserved.

I loved every moment we spent together and the dinners we enjoyed
Every Friday at Posa Posa in Nanuet.
Our memories at St. Ann's can never be destroyed
As they are held in high esteem still yet.

You wore the collar well, Monsignor;
You are a legend for your love and dedication.
I want you to know that your memory will last with me forever
And your lessons will always be reflected in my testament and vocation.

A Note About God Bless America

I am sure that everyone remembers where he or she was when this horrific event occurred. This was surreal, and I remember finding it difficult to comprehend the monstrosity that it was. The enmity that inspired such a ludicrous act was hard to swallow; the worst of the human condition had once again reared its ugly head. The American spirit, however, is one to be proud of; in fact, I believe it to be incomparable. We are founded upon the same principles of Arthur and our freedoms are the closest we come to Camelot on this great earth. Once again, it is time to turn the page and allow the human spirit to triumph while our banner continues to fly high.

God Bless America

May God bless America
For all that it seems;
It challenges the human spirit
To manifest dreams.

On that horrid day in September
That wretched morning of 9-1-1,
We remember the enmity that caused
The loss of our daughters and sons.

Each morning offers new beginnings;
Every person starts anew,
Working in perfect measure
To make all dreams come true.

It is the turning of the page
Where one finds solace,
Erasing images of horror
Born from hatred and malice.

We are reminded from time to time
Through moments of tribulation and terror
That our banner will continue to fly
And our freedoms will last forever.

Conviction
Poems for a Stalwart Spirit

When we love, we experience;
when we experience, we learn;
when we learn, we grow;
when we grow, we become.
And when we become, we fulfill that
potential of ourselves which is all
that we can be: Love.

A Note About Summit

I enjoyed writing Summit. Hope is a vital component in our lives and when we embrace it we find that it often leads to positive action. I believe we despair when we feel there is no hope. In many instances hope is all that we have. And in many cases hope is all that we need to springboard us to success, happiness and fulfillment. We can expect the best from ourselves, there is nothing wrong with that. After all, what else is there? When we push ourselves to the limit, we are often surprised at what we can accomplish. We are of the human condition, and we are made in the image and likeness of God; therefore, our potential is unlimited. So, keep reaching, the stars are not out of sight.

Summit

Keep climbing, the summit is attainable.
Don't give in, think all things are possible.
No retreat;
No defeat.
Believe in the unbelievable.

Keep reaching, the stars are not out of sight.
Reach farther, never give up the fight.
Do not regress;
Don't acquiesce.
Believe everything will be alright.

Keep dreaming, your wishes are not far away.
Keep hoping, your dreams may come true today.
Do not resist;
Simply persist.
Believe your footsteps know the way.

A Note About Dusk To Dawn

The idea came to me after watching the morning news how people can often lead double lives, presenting one image of themselves in daylight and another under the moonlight, although often at a price. I decided to tell that story. Then I decided to tell this in a way that would be challenging for myself. I began with a one syllable word. Then a word with two ... and so on up until I reached eight syllables. In the end I came up with a story about the risks of leading double lives and how each day dawn offers a second chance.

Dusk to Dawn

Dusk
Twilight
Temptation
Apprehension
Determination
Only integrity
Can offer serenity
When the plight needs strong resistance.
Night
Opaque
Concealing
Unforgiving
Demoralizing
Grants wishes to sinners;
A black hole for beginners,
Innocence tainted by circumstance.
Dawn
Rising
Promising
Optimistic
Opportunistic
A new hope for dreamers;
Redemption for believers,
Contrition and a second chance.

A Note About When Married

In an earlier note I mentioned how ideas for poems can come to you in a variety of ways, often in your sleep. In this case it was virtually no different. One morning I awoke to find a tune in my head. It was one line ... mother is in the upstairs room, she dallies. Now I do not know about the rest of you, but I do not find myself often using the word dallies in my speech. Nevertheless, my rejoinder in jest was ... okay, father is in the downstairs room ... he tallies. Immediately a voice sprang in my head with ... one enjoys the morning rain. I related that to the former line with mother and so I answered, the other yearns for the afternoon game. Immediately the voice replied with the next line and I followed in rhyme ending the game. I found this hysterical and so I continued with the second stanza. However this game started I was pleased with the end result. I do not know where the voice came from, but I appreciated the game. I love this little poem because of how it came to be. It does tell the story of how love grows between two people despite the individuality of both.

When Married

mother is in the upstairs room,
she dallies.
father is in the downstairs room,
he tallies.
one enjoys the morning rain;
the other yearns for the afternoon game.
in the end it's all the same,
when married.

mother wonders about the darkening sky,
she withers.
father aimlessly wanders by,
he dithers.
one is concerned whether the children will come;
the other prays for the afternoon sun.
despite diverging thoughts they are one,
together.

A Note About Unbreakable

Unbreakable came at a time in my life when I felt challenged and threatened by what I perceived to be enemies all around me. I think many of you can relate to this feeling. I think ego gets in the way for all of us sometimes. What is important is that we remember our focus and keep steady our resolve during difficult times. We need to believe in ourselves. It is all about conviction. I believed in myself during this trying time in my life and that made all the difference. This is the longest poem I have written; it's separated into three parts. The first stanza tells the story in third person, the second stanza is like the Council of the Elder who speaks on your behalf because it knows you better, and the third stanza is my conviction and belief in myself—it is my voice. I begin and end the poem with Unbreakable. We all have something to offer this world; do not let others judge and treat you cruelly! Protect your dignity and integrity—no one else will do it for you! Be firm in your beliefs and in the fact that you too are Unbreakable.

Unbreakable (Part One)

From where he stands he is a man against the world.
He is challenged by the heights of Everest and Kilimanjaro.
Yet, there is strength and faith in this solitary figure,
And he will not tremble and surrender in sorrow.

Your attempts to cause his annihilation
Only fuels his fire and determination.
He will shield his heart from your calumny,
And he will conquer this wave of adversity.

"I am
Unbreakable, Indomitable
Your lies will not torment my soul.
Immovable, Indestructible
My will and resolve keeps me whole."

Unbreakable (Part Two)

From the deck this captain witnesses his crew
Engage in evil, deceit and blasphemy.
Yet, there is an unwavering spirit in this lone seafarer,
Despite the collective dissension and mutiny.

Your efforts to treat him with castigation
Will only lead to the ship's own desolation.
And he will weather the winds of anarchy
And coast on the currents of victory.

"I am
Unflappable, Impenetrable
You have failed in your attempts at control.
Undeniable, Unforgettable
I have succeeded in my leadership role."

Unbreakable (Part Three)

Alone against his critics he faces unyielding scorn;
He is assailed with vicious slander and scrutiny.
Yet, there are limitless depths of perseverance in this leader,
And he will not cave in to such actions of cruelty.

You use malice as your ammunition
To ignite internal conflagration.
But he will ignore your shameful mockery
And the sounds of silent cacophony.

"I am
Incredible, Unbelievable
I am a victim whose story is untold.
Unshakable, Unbreakable
I'm an innocent whose heart is pure gold."

A Note About Fight Fire With Fire

This is a tribute to the horror genre which I love. It was sparked when my son Timothy came into the den and pointed to a VHS tape of Phantasm with the Tall Man. My wife and I laughed about our little two year old son who was able to recognize the creature in this movie. I love this series; it's my favorite. Anyway, I began thinking of all the monsters we grew up with and decided to write this poem as a tribute to the things that keep us up at night.

I know many of you can relate. The poem was written as I sat at the computer within five minutes. It was fun!

Fight Fire With Fire

I am going to yield to my desires
Fight fire with fire
And make history!
I am going to admit no defeat
turn up the heat
and claim victory!

I am going to take your best shots
Give you all I've got
And leave you far behind!
I am going to leave you pleading
Incessantly bleeding
With so little time!

I am going to leave you breathless
Be ever relentless
With no pity!
I am going to stake my claim
With fortune and fame
In every city!

I am going to leave you frail
On this torturous trail
Of destruction!
I am going to bend your will
And leave you still
In devastation!

I am going to leave you forgotten
A corpse so rotten
In ambiguity!
I am going to remember your face
Leave little to trace
For posterity!

A Note About
A Tribute To Mankind

The idea for A Tribute to Mankind probably came to me during one of my existentialist meltdowns. Despite what I perceive to be a solid foundation in my faith, I do wonder from time to time about what happens next. Don't we all? Well, we will never have the answers. I decided to stop wasting time on questions without answers and began dwelling instead on all of the possibilities. If we all had the desire to shape new paradigms! I love the quote by William Blake: "Great things are done when men and mountains meet." Substitute women as well. Isn't that great, though? The poem starts slowly and races to a finish. I hope you like it.

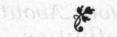

A Tribute to Mankind

If the water we drink is
the same water shared by dinosaurs,
then doesn't that make you
wonder about who we are?
Are we simply matter
re-defined, re-formed, re-shaped?
With a future as bleak as
the worst that we can imagine,
and with tomorrow's days devoid of promise,
I feel no more importance as that of anonymous.
And with this fate shaping my eternity
I can only state with brevity:
That I shall not waste one minute on minutiae!
Instead, I shall chase the winds and the sands of time,
define my own course, and shape new paradigms.
I shall change the course of human history
and effort to discover life's greatest mysteries.
I shall leave a trail that leads one to find
a glorious destination and a tribute to mankind.

A Note About Definition

We define ourselves by our journey. As Joseph Campbell puts it: "We make the road by walking it." We often hear life described as a journey rather than a destination. I believe that many of us spend too much time looking for the road map instead of understanding that growth occurs when we travel to unknown destinations. When we risk we expose ourselves to new experiences. In truth, each day we enter the unknown; we never know from day to day what is in store for us. Only our previous conceptions of past experiences limit our understanding of the present moment, and they often frighten us about the future and endless possibilities. Be stalwart, and define yourself at every turn!

Definition

*Only mirrors
can lead one to see
the vision behind
one man's identity.*

*Only reflections
can bring understanding
in defining one's voice
in proportionate meaning.*

*Only images
of achievable conditions
guide many to journey,
determining definition.*

A Note About Reverse the Trend

My wife likes this poem and wanted it to be last. I like it, too. So, my friends, it is last in the book. Many of you can relate to this poem. It tells the same story as Demonstratives. Sometimes fate lends us a cruel hand and we have to find our own way home. This is when we rely on faith, family and friends to guide us. Many thanks to all of the people who have been there for us during our times of trouble. Believe me when I tell you that you will never be forgotten, each and every one of you. We are grateful and we love you all.

Reverse the Trend

It's funny how I feel today.
My dreams have fluttered and flown away.
My hope and happiness were led astray.
I've seen better days.

It's this career thing again.
Seems I turned onto another dead end.
When will it ever end?
Will good luck and fortune ever blend?

I've been stretching my thinking to the limit.
Why can't I play the game for once and win it?
It's exhausting being in constant transit.
Destiny has become a cruel bandit!

Oh, well. Time to move on,
Sing a different song,
Be persistent and stay strong.
Don't others let on!

The rainbow has another end.
My misery will soon be on the mend.
Faith will be my trustworthy friend.
This is how I will reverse the trend.

The Lord's Room

Last night an angel of the Lord appeared to me in a dream and asked, "What would you say if I gave you a large room and told you that you would be kept to this one room for life everlasting?" "Well," I said with trust, "Praise be to God!" The angel continued, "And if I asked you to furnish this room, what would you say then?" Again I replied in faith, "Praise be to God!"

Before answering further, I pondered, knowing that my faith in my Lord was being tested. Therefore, trying to understand the motives implied, I replied in jest: "First, I would ask the Lord to come and stay with me. The Lord is my life-giving source, my spiritual food, and the light of my world. I would also ask him to be my armchair because, like the Lord, an armchair represents open arms.

Second, I would ask the Holy Spirit to be with me. The Spirit of the Lord is my comforter and my life-giving water. He speaks and pleads on my behalf when I am unable to do so. Certainly, he can be my pillow.

Next, My wife and eternal soul mate would be the love that permeates my room for eternity. Together and forever we will enliven and illuminate the room with the bonds that unite us. She would be the music playing softly and the candles burning brightly.

I would fill the rest of the room with my children. They are my energy and happiness. My children are my every heart beat! They represent youthfulness and vitality. They would be my music and my alarm clock, a constant reminder of how young at heart we ought to be.

I would have my parents and family there with me. They represent warmth, caring, compassion, and understanding, as well as all of my fondest memories. My parents and family would be the pictures on my walls.

Finally, I would also welcome my friends in for they represent joy, togetherness, and laughter. They would make up my 'living room' for sure!

Oh, and I would paint the walls with love!"

The angel smiled and said, "So be it then."

Confused, I asked "What will become of this room? Will you indeed present this room to me? And the angel of the Lord spoke in reply, "You already possess this room. Your body already holds within itself this very room I speak of; it is the Lord's temple—His room. You see, child of God, you will find your room where you find your heart!"

I paused and thought for a moment.

"Praise be to God!"

Acknowledgements

I wish to thank my Lord, Jesus Christ, for his divine inspiration. I could not have done this without his thoughts and those of the Holy Spirit.

I wish to thank my beautiful, loving wife Alicia for her inspiration and support throughout the years and during the making of this book. I Love You, my Princess!

Very special thanks to my wonderful children: Sarah, Eugene, Daniel, Timothy, and Elizabeth. This book is for you! I love each and every one of you with all of my heart. I hope you enjoy this forever.

Very special thanks to my parents, Elizabeth and Eugene (I know you're here with me, Dad!). No words could ever describe how much I love you both. You are wonderful role models and the best parents children could ever have.

Thank you to my sisters Karen and Nancy and to my wonderful nieces and nephews: Corey, Carlos, Kiah and Calista. It's your turn to shine!

Thank you to my wonderful and supportive in-laws and second family: Dick and Judy, Donna and John, Emily, Elaine, Amanda, Lauren, John Jr., Julianne, George and Cindy, Great Grandma Bertha Monkovic.

Thank you to all of my extended family for being there when my mother needed you most this past year when we lost our father. I love my extended family; I am proud of all of them. Special thank you to Uncle Jackie and Aunt Yvette, Uncle Eddie and Aunt Debbie, Aunt Margaret and Bob, Aunt Dottie, Jamie, Terry, Tara and Arthur, Ricky and Darlene, Uncle Billy and Aunt Dee Dee, Uncle Jimmy W., Jackie and Debbie, Joey and Luanne, Uncle Joey and Aunt Josette, Audrey and Brian, Bill and Jeannie, Michelle and Patrick, Dutchie and Virginia, Rose, Uncle Pete and Aunt Harriet, Frankie, Tony, Debbie, Cathy, Stephanie, Robbie, Freddy and Peggy, Sherry, Billy W, Freddie C., Louise and Nelson, and B.P.O.E. #877. I wish I could name all of you here.

Special thanks to my friends who were there for me during my difficult moments: Bob, Jose, Bruce, Stephanie, Joan, Sally, Janie, Scott B, and Anne-Renee.

A very special, heartfelt thank you to those who helped keep us alive for close to two years: Sr. Helen, Rich, Mary Lou, Laura, Michelena, Sr. Barbara, Maureen, Margaret, Deacon Peter, Sr. Stephen, Sr. Joanne, Father Al, and Monsignor Corrigan, Ursula, Sr. Theresa, Sr. Jessica, Mrs. More, Mrs. Mimi.

Special thanks to Orange-Ulster BOCES for their overwhelming compassion and support: June, Marijane, Maria, Mariann, Marie K., Bob M, Jim, Bob D, Don, Sonia, Cheryl, Barbara, Regina, Jonathan, Veronique, Kevin, Yesenia, Gene A., and Tom.

A very special thank you to Molly Gabbard, my Publishing Services Associate, for making my publishing experience such a pleasure, and for her patience and attention to detail. Thank you, Molly.

For those I may have missed, thank you so very much! Enjoy!

To Tom Jones, thank you for being a friend. You will not be forgotten.

About the Author

<u>My Gift To You: A Collection of Poetry on Love, Loss and Life</u> is Eugene T. Hewitt, Jr's first book of poetry. Although this is Mr. Hewitt's first anthology of his work, his poems have been published in books since 1987. He is an experienced Educator of more than two decades and has been both a teacher and administrator. His poetry, quotations and notes are poignant reflections on all that it means to be human. His poetry and candor should resonate with all who appreciate the art. He welcomes your feedback and hopes you enjoy his gift to you.

978-0-595-51393-2
0-595-51393-X

CPSIA information can be obtained
at www.ICGtesting.com
Printed in the USA
LVHW031034290423
745661LV00031B/1074